GIRLS GUIDES

From Algebra to Zits:

A Girl's Guide to Making the Most of Life at School

Jeanne Strazzabosco

the rosen publishing group's
rosen central
new york

I would like to thank Girls of Pride and all the very special girls at Pittsford Middle School. Thank you for your time and thoughtful reflections. Your positive outlook and enthusiasm inspire me more than you'll ever know. Keep on dreaming. Thanks also to my daughters. You are food for my soul.

Published in 2000 by The Rosen Publishing Group, Inc.
29 East 21st Street, New York, NY 10010

First Edition

Library of Congress Cataloging-in-Publication Data

Strazzabosco, Jeanne.
        From algebra to zits : a girl's guide to life at school/ by
        Jeanne Strazzabosco.
            p.   cm. — (Girls guides)
        Includes bibliographical references (p. 45) and index.
        Summary: Presents information and advice for girls in middle school on a variety of subjects from Algebra and Guys to Periods & Puberty and Zits.
        ISBN 0-8239-2983-3
        1. Teenage girls—Education (Middle school) Juvenile literature. 2. Middle school students—Conduct of life Juvenile literature. [1. Teenage girls. 2. Conduct of life.] I. Title.   II. Series.
        LB36607.S76   1999
        372.18—dc21
                                                                                            99-37475
                                                                                            CIP

Manufactured in the United States of America

Contents

About This Book

The middle school years are like a roller coaster—wild and scary but also fun and way cool. One minute you're way, way up there, and the next minute you're plunging down into the depths. Not surprisingly, sometimes you may find yourself feeling confused and lost. Not to worry, though. Just like on a roller-coaster ride, at the end of all this crazy middle school stuff, you'll be laughing and screaming and talking about how awesome it all was.

Right now, however, chances are your body is changing so much that it's barely recognizable, your old friends may not share your interests anymore, and your life at school is suddenly hugely complicated. And let's not even get into the whole boy issue. It's a wonder that you can still think straight at all.

Fortunately, reader dear, help is here. This book is your road map. It's also a treasure chest filled with ideas and advice. Armed with this book and with your own inner strength (trust us, you have plenty), you can safely, confidently navigate the twists and turns of your middle school years. It will be tough going, and sometimes you'll wonder if you'll ever get through it. But you—fabulous, powerful, unique you—are up to the task. This book is just a place to start.

Welcome to Middle School!

If you've picked up this book, you are probably between ten and fourteen years old. You've said farewell to the warm hugs, scented stickers, straight lines, and cupcake parties of elementary school. You are ready for middle school, a fantastic time of new learning and fun, change and opportunity. You'll make new friends, join clubs, learn how to follow a schedule, and move about school on your own.

The following sections are designed to help you explore the many aspects of being a girl in middle school. Read this book as if it were written by an older sister who has already successfully navigated the waters of middle school. You will learn how to cope with everything from locker combinations and class schedules to algebra and zits. In short, you'll learn how to make the most of life in middle school.

Algebra

Is Math Important? You Betcha.

When girls hit their teens, many of them lose interest in math and begin to struggle with the subject. Many girls begin to think it's not cool to be smart in math anymore (science, too!), and they stand aside while the boys have the success and earn good math grades.

Math is not a "guy" thing. Math is for everyone. It is a magical language of numbers and symbols that both girls and boys can learn to speak, with great benefits for the future. Make math your friend. Girls who want to have challenging and rewarding careers in the future—as engineers, or as doctors, or in many areas of business—need to work to earn good grades in math.

Realize that you'll make mistakes as you work to solve math problems. The more you practice, the better you'll become. If you need help, ask

your math teacher or another student. It might be a great way to start a new friendship. You and your friends could even agree to work together to help each other out.

Bodies & Beauty

The media, especially the entertainment industry, sends the message that all girls should be a size four and wear two pounds of makeup and hair products. Listen carefully: That is not reality.

It's normal to wonder about your body and your looks, but it's important to be realistic and not be swayed by the images you see on TV, in movies, and in magazines. Those people make their living by looking a particular way. They're paid to look like that. But you'll profit most by being comfortable with who you are.

Your body is going through some major changes right now. Most girls will have their first period during the middle school years. Your breasts are beginning to develop; your straight lines are becoming curvy. If you're uncomfortable with these changes, look around.

You're not alone—no matter what you're feeling. A friend of mine went into a deep panic the first time she had to wear a bra. For weeks she wore an old undershirt over it so nobody would see it! Crazy, maybe, but a normal reaction.

Your body and your appearance might be sources of frustration for you, but take heed of this simple advice: Hating the way you look NEVER makes you more attractive, but self-confidence and self-respect are always in style.

Computers

Computers Aren't Just for Playing Games?

In the future, most jobs and careers will undoubtedly require knowledge of technology, especially computers. It's never too early to start honing your skills. Even if you don't have a computer at home, you may be able to use computers at school or at the public library.

Some middle schools

even offer computer courses for their students. One practical and useful application is word processing. Teachers often require their students to type their reports and projects instead of handwriting them.

There are some user-friendly computer applications that you can use to make exciting presentations and reports. These applications will let you record your voice, music, or sound effects. You can insert pictures, diagrams, or graphs.

Your school librarian will also know which CD-ROMs are available for research. Entire encyclopedias, atlases, and magazine and newspaper articles can be found on CD-ROMs. In addition to written text, you'll find video clips, photographs, and audio clips.

Diversity

Doesn't Everyone Celebrate Christmas?

Making friends with someone whose background and culture are different from your own is a great way to make your world larger. Such friendships will teach you to respect and appreciate differences. These friendships will help you grow and prepare yourself for the diverse world you'll enter in the future.

Think about your group of friends. How diverse is it? Do all your friends look and sound just like you? Do you have a friend who speaks a language other than English at home? A friend who was born in another country? How about a friend whose parents come from a foreign country?

Do you have a friend who practices a different religion? One who is physically challenged? Deaf or blind? One whose skin is a different color than yours?

Education

Do We Really Get to Change Classes?

In elementary school, you probably stayed in the same classroom with the same teacher for most of the day. All right, maybe you changed rooms for art, music, or gym.

Middle school will be different. In middle school, you'll change classes every forty minutes or so and have eight or nine different teachers. The day will begin in homeroom, where attendance will be taken and various announcements will be made. Then it's on to your first class.

You will most likely be required to take math, science, English, and social studies. You will probably also be able to choose from other courses that interest you. These courses are usually called electives, and they might include such things as art, band, chorus, computers, foreign languages, journalism, and drama. The purpose of electives is to let you explore subjects that interest you. Electives can also be the start of a lifelong interest that influences what career you ultimately choose.

In addition, you may have a study hall a couple of times a week. Study hall is a quiet time in a supervised classroom where you can study for a quiz, do the required reading for your classes, or get a head start on your homework.

Friends

What If My Best Friend Isn't in Any of My Classes?

In middle school, you will meet and be in classes with kids from several different elementary schools. Your friends from elementary school

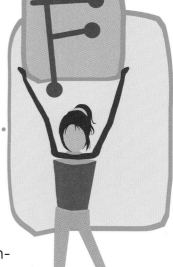

will still be important to you, but you'll start to form new friendships as well. Trust me; I guarantee it.

Meeting new people, making new friends, and finding new and different activities that you like to do can be enormously exciting. But a time when people are trying out new friendships is also a time when it is easy for feelings to get hurt. Some of your old friends may feel like they are being left out of your new friendships and activities. They may feel as if they aren't as important or special to you any more. Or you may find yourself feeling the same way, as your old friends start doing new things.

One way to deal with these complications is to try hard to be a good friend. Here are some guidelines that will always be helpful:

 Don't gossip or talk about your friends behind their back. If you have a problem with something they did or said, talk to them about it. Be honest, and tell them how you feel.

 Be trustworthy. If a friend tells you something that she wants kept a secret, like that she thinks the new boy

in math is cute, don't blab it to the world. How would you feel if she did that to you? A friend is someone you can trust not to do stuff like that.

 But if a friend is in some kind of serious trouble, you need to get advice from an adult. If a friend tells you something in confidence that worries or troubles you—especially something that affects her health, safety, or well-being—it is okay to talk to an adult about it.

 Be a good listener. Don't just listen to the words; listen for the feelings behind the words. Sometimes it is difficult for people to express exactly what they need to in words alone. Be an open and sympathetic listener.

 Be honest. Never lie to a friend.

 Be supportive. Help a friend with a homework assignment, go to her soccer match and cheer her on, share your lunch if she forgets hers at home, and decorate her locker for her birthday. Cheer her up when she's down; congratulate her when she accomplishes something important to her.

 Encourage your friends to do their very best.

One Minute They're Cute, the Next They're Totally Gross.

There are bound to be times—probably lots of them—when you'll be confused and even frustrated by what boys say and do. However, friendships with boys can also be fun and meaningful. A middle school girl recently shared the following with me: "Sometimes I just don't get boys. I was talking to a boy the other day and he walked away before I was even finished talking."

Hard as it may be for you to believe, it might be helpful to remember that most boys experience times—a lot of times—when they are frustrated and confused by what girls say and do. Girls and boys are both going through some pretty major changes at this age, changes that can cause them to do some pretty goofy things sometimes. Everyone is really just trying to figure out who and how he or she wants to be. You might be dealing with wearing your first bra; boys are struggling with their voices changing and cracking when they least expect it.

But what can be said about relationships with guys in middle school? Here's a classic scene that takes place in the halls of middle schools everywhere, every day: "Carrie, find out if Adam likes me. Don't tell him that I like him unless he says he likes me first, okay?"

As a former middle school girl, I can tell you that a conversation like this is a big waste of time. It's tempting to gossip sometimes. In fact, it might seem like the main way girls and boys talk to and about each other. Most of the time the note-passing stuff is harmless, but words can and do cause hurt feelings and misunderstandings. As in all situations, the best way to deal with people is clearly and honestly. Not to mention that talking directly to a boy is a far better way of getting his attention than whispering behind his back.

Healthy Lifestyle

Yeah, but Everyone Is Doing It.

In the United States, young girls are now the fastest growing group of new smokers. Maybe billboard and magazine advertisements, or peer pressure, are to blame for this increase, but an advertisement doesn't buy a pack of cigarettes, smoke them, and share them with friends. It's young girls, a lot like you, who do the smoking.

It is never too soon to start thinking about how you are going to maintain a healthy lifestyle. And health includes more than just your body—it includes your body, your spirit, and your mind. Being healthy means taking care of yourself physically, mentally, and emotionally.

You already have the most important part of what you need to take care of yourself. Whether you call it your conscience, your heart, or your inner voice, the same thing that tells you right from wrong can help you turn your back on cigarette smoking, drinking alcohol, using drugs, or other risky behaviors. What you need—the strength and courage to be yourself, and to do what is best for you—is already inside you. And don't be afraid to talk to an adult about any of this. It can be a parent, teacher, or a counselor, just so long as it is someone you know you can trust. It may be just what you need.

Independence

I'll Be up in My Room.

Adolescence is a time of growing and testing the boundaries. You're starting to feel the lure of independence. Your friendships are vitally important to you as well. A lot of the time,

you'd probably rather be at the mall with a friend instead of eating dinner with your family. But as you head to your bedroom to put on your favorite CD, consider this: You need your family, and they need you. You're a team. When one of the players on a team is down, the rest of the team rallies for support. The team wants to cheer during the exciting moments as well.

Your relationship with your family is even more important now. Keep the lines of communication open at home. Share the ups and downs of your day with your parents and brothers and sisters. Find time each day to talk. Plan special family activities once a week, like board game night or video and popcorn night.

Be open-minded when it comes to your parents and their wishes and feelings. Trust what they know and have already lived through. Believe it or not, they actually know some things that might help you. And if your family seems too busy with their own lives to listen to you, don't get too discouraged, and don't give up. It is just possible that they think you want a little more "space" than you used to, and this is their way of giving it to you. Keep reaching out.

I'm Never Going to Use Any of This Stuff Anyhow, Right?

In school, you learn skills that you will use for the rest of your life. Your learning experiences today will provide you with skills that you'll need for a future job or career. And it's not all just about your schoolwork, in class or at home. What you learn about getting along with and working with people can be just as important to your future.

When you work in a group on a project, do you cooperate as best you can to get the job done? Do you try to find ways to contribute? Or do you sit back and let others do the work? Good teamwork requires group members who share the responsibilities equally, cooperate, and dedicate themselves to the task at hand.

Communication skills and the ability to work well with others is vital to success in virtually every aspect of life, especially on the job or in a career. Be open-minded and non-

$E=MC^2$

judgmental when listening to other people's ideas. Realize that working together with someone is often the way to find the best possible solution to a problem.

Deadlines are a crucial part of most jobs and careers. By consistently handing in your school assignments on time, you're learning to meet deadlines as well as developing the totally important skill of time management.

Spend a day at work with a parent to witness firsthand the skills he or she uses daily. An awesome tradition that has been established in recent years is "Take Your Daughter to Work Day." On this day, which is celebrated in the spring, thousands of young women across the United States shadow a parent or mentor on the job.

Knowledge

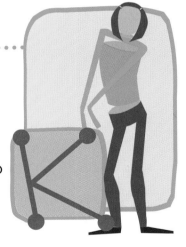

Is It All About Grades?

Sometimes students, teachers, and parents get so caught up in As, Bs, and Cs that they forget about the real reason that children go to school: to learn. And there is a lot more to learning than just getting a better grade than somebody else.

Knowledge is the finest gift your teachers have to offer. Use your time in school to become a seeker of knowledge. Take advantage of this time. Be curious and eager. Find things that interest you. Get your hand in the air and ask questions.

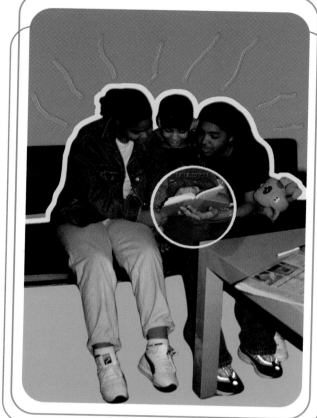

Read, and think about things. Share your ideas and opinions in classroom discussion. Let your teachers see your excitement. Talk with your friends about the things that interest you. Read a newspaper each day and keep up with what is going on in the world outside your school and your home. Talk to your parents about current events. Seek out as many worthwhile opinions as possible about the things and subjects that interest you.

If you try your hardest and set meaningful goals, you'll never have anything to fear from the land of As, Bs, and Cs. And believe it or not, the very best thing you can get by becoming a seeker of knowledge may not even be good grades, a sense of accomplishment and self-worth, and a bright future, even though all those things are very important.

What is the most valuable gift you'll receive by developing your curiosity, by becoming a seeker of knowledge? You will never, ever be bored.

Lockers

We Get to Have Lockers!

Lockers line the halls of just about every middle school in America, and brand new middle schoolers cannot wait to have one of their very own.

On your first day of school, you will be assigned a locker. At the same time, you will be given a three-number combination to the lock on your locker, if it has one, or you may be asked to bring a combination padlock from home.

At middle school, all of your belongings will be kept in your locker—your books, notebooks, coat, lunch, boots, hat, gloves, sports equipment, and more. You don't want other people helping themselves to your bologna sandwich or your math homework, do you? If not, it is probably best to keep it locked up. Keep your belongings safe by keeping your locker locked between classes, and only give your combination to people you trust completely.

Before they begin middle school, some students worry about using a locker. Mainly, they worry about being able to use the lock, especially if they have not used a combination lock before. They worry that they won't be able to get the lock open, or that they will forget the combination, or that the whole thing will take them too long in the few minutes they have before classes.

Don't worry about this too much, and don't worry too much about worrying. These fears are natural, and probably every student has had them at one time or another, even if they do not like to admit it. I did once, and today, many years later, I can still remember my combination from middle school: 19–21–22. It was easy to remember because my birthday was on the 19th of March, and my brother's was on the 22nd. But you'll find your own ways to memorize your combination. One good way to address these fears is simply to practice using a combination lock outside of school.

Before you know it, your locker will feel as comfortable to you as your own bedroom—a combination library, mailbox, hangout for friends, and clothes drawer. But it is a very good idea to keep in mind these famous words proclaimed by my seventh-grade English teacher: "A well-organized locker is a sign of a successful student." This is as true today as it was then. If you keep your books and school supplies neatly organized, you will be able to easily locate what you need for your next class and make it there with time to spare. That is, of course, if only that darn lock will open!

Management & Making It Work

How Am I Ever Going to Remember All This Stuff?

When you buy school supplies, be sure to pick up a calendar or planner. Select one that has plenty of writing space for each day. Put your daily schedule on the first page, along with class times and room numbers. This will be very handy the first few weeks of school.

As you go through your school day, keep your calendar with you. As your teachers give you assignments, write them down under the day they're due. Write down the assignment clearly. Sometimes kids write down "work sheet" or "write a paragraph," and then forget exactly what it is they are supposed to do by the time they get home.

When your teacher gives you a long-term assignment—one that is not due for

a few weeks—do not put it off until the last minute. Break up the assignment into smaller pieces. For example, if you have a research paper due on the causes of the Civil War, you could do the research the first week. The second week, you could write the rough draft. The week before it is due, complete the rewrites and the bibliography.

Nurture Yourself

But Pizza and Ice Cream Are My Favorite Foods!

The two most important things you can do for yourself are to eat well-balanced meals and stay physically active. Keep the junk food and the hours dazed out in front of a computer screen or television to a minimum. Cut back on your TV sit-com consumption and use the time to take a bike ride or play a game of kickball with some friends.

Be sensible when it comes to the food in the school cafeteria. Unfortunately, many school cafeterias offer lunches high in fat. If the entree for the day is loaded with fat, opt for a cup of soup and a sandwich. Be sure to round off your lunch with a piece of fruit as well.

When making your lunch at home, throw in some carrot sticks in addition to the Oreos. Toss in a banana besides the chips. You must give your body healthy food so that it can keep you energized through your busy day.

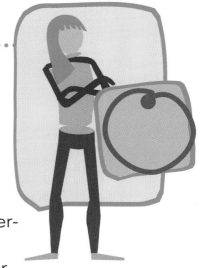

Sleep is also an important consideration. Your body is changing and growing. Eight hours of sleep a night is vital to your well-being.

Optimize Your Potential

Study? What Does That Mean?

Here are some helpful tips from girls who have learned how to achieve academic success in middle school. These girls understand that many of the skills they're learning now will affect the way the rest of their lives unfold.

 Keep a calendar or planner in which you write all your homework assignments.

 Find a quiet study area in your home. Make sure that you're away from ringing telephones and TV shows.

Sit at a table or desk to do your work. If you lie on your bed to study, particularly if you're tired out from all your other activities, you'll fall asleep in no time at all.

 Make room in your busy schedule for homework by using your calendar or daily planner to plan study hours and phone time with your pals. Make sure your nightly chat with your best friend doesn't conflict with your schoolwork.

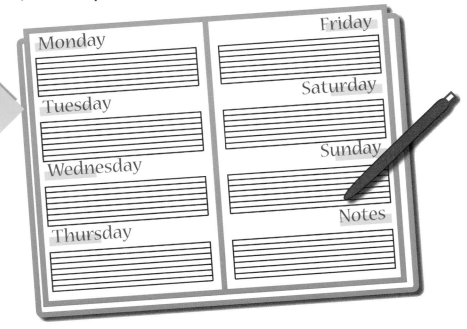

Monday

Tuesday

Wednesday

Thursday

Friday

Saturday

Sunday

Notes

 Don't procrastinate, meaning don't put things off until later. You'll seriously regret it at 9 PM the night before your five-page essay is due and you haven't even written your outline yet!

Color stimulates the brain, so try copying your notes with colored markers.

 Make yourself flash cards on topics or subjects you're trying to master, and ask a family member to quiz you.

 Try making a recording of yourself explaining key concepts. Listen to the tape as you ride or walk to school.

 Form study groups with your friends and help each other study—make sure you do actually study.

Periods & Puberty

Why Am I Taller than All the Boys?

If you're a sixth-grade girl, you may have noticed that many of the girls are taller than the boys. This growth spurt is normal and is one of the first signs of puberty for girls. Girls enter puberty earlier than boys. During puberty, special chemicals called hormones are released by your glands. They tell your body that it is time to make some changes. For example, your breasts begin to develop, and you grow hair in your armpits and pubic area, the hair on your legs darkens.

Hormones also signal your reproductive organs that it is time to begin to develop. Once your reproductive organs have developed, you will get your first period, or menstruation. It's tricky to know exactly when this will happen, because girls develop at different rates. Some may start menstruating as young as nine, while others may not start until they're sixteen. One thing is for sure: Your first period won't start until your breasts have begun to develop or your pubic hair has started to grow. If these changes have not begun for you, you probably will have to wait a little while longer before you experience your first period.

Question

Hey! Does Anybody Hear Me?

Studies show that girls often let themselves be silenced when they hit their teenage years or adolescence. In other words, girls of ten or eleven are confident, freely share their opinions and ideas, and eagerly question the world around them. But around the age of thirteen, many begin to lose confidence and to doubt themselves. They stop allowing themselves to be as curious or as bold as they were before.

For example, a thirteen-year-old girl and her ten-year-old sister were taking a ceramics class. The younger girl asked many questions about how to do various things, had tons of ideas about what she wanted to make, and was proud of all her projects. The thirteen year old sat quietly, once in a while complaining that she didn't know what to do, and said she hated everything she made in the class. Don't miss out on fun and inspiring experiences by being silent. Let your voice be heard at every age. Ask questions and seek answers that make sense to you. Stand up for yourself and be confident in what you know and feel.

Renew

I'm Only Thirteen Years Old. I Don't Need to Recharge My Battery.

Taking a nap is not the only way you can recharge your personal batteries. To make the most out of every day, you need to pay attention to four aspects of life: your physical, mental, and spiritual well-being and your relationships with others. All four of these areas need to be recharged regularly so that you can be the best that you can be.

Renew yourself physically by exercising. Exercise can consist of anything from playing a team sport to walking instead of getting a ride. Physical exercise is a fun way to relax and unwind after school.

Mental renewal comes from reading or from writing in a journal. Consider cutting back on some of your television watching, and read a book or magazine simply for pleasure. Writing in a journal or diary is an excellent way to express your feelings.

You renew your spirit when you connect with the things you treasure the most. Climbing trees, playing with your dog, writing to a grandparent, collecting sea-shells, and listening to music are examples of how you might renew your spirit.

Lastly, be sure to take care of your relationships with family and friends. Clear the dinner table without being asked, send a cheerful note to a friend, walk the dog even though it's your brother's turn, or surprise your mom and dad by making them lunch.

The Social Life

I'll Meet You at the Mall!

The biggest show in town is playing this week: It's your social life, and you don't want to miss it.

There is so much to do at your age. You have friends to keep up with, shopping at the mall, movies, and parties on the weekend. Dances, games, and concerts abound. You want to be cool and popular, and you want to do it all! So, um, what about homework?

The trick you've got to learn in middle school, which will help you blast through high school and college in a blaze of glory, is BALANCE.

In order to make the most of your education and still have a fabulous time, you've got to balance your social life and your school work. Don't blow off reading your lit assignment to go to the mall. But by the same token, don't think that succeeding in school is an all-or-nothing deal. You don't have to glue a book to your face to be a good student. Life is about learning, and learning comes from classes, books, and teachers as well as from your friends, peers, and experiences.

The easiest way to achieve this magical balance is to surround yourself with people who value their education and value each other. You just might find that your friends can actually help you to be a great student, and that being serious about school is a great way to make friends.

Teachers

Whose Side Are They on, Anyhow?

Teachers are special people. They have chosen as their life's work to help young people learn. You have to admit, that's pretty cool. Each day your teachers prepare activities to help you along your path of learning, whether the subject is social studies or art. If you're having trouble in a particular area, ask your teachers for help. They'll find time for you, even if it's during lunch or after school.

Come to class ready to learn, and participate in classroom discussions. Learning is way more fun when you take an active role by asking questions and sharing your ideas. And teachers have an easier time making the class interesting and challenging when they have a good idea what their students are interested in. Your learning is an important project for both you and your teachers. So talk to them: After all, you're on the same team!

Teachers also want to help their students become good citizens. The classroom is a place where young people learn how to cooperate with and be respectful of all different kinds of people, and teachers are there to make sure this happens.

Lastly, if you are troubled by something a teacher says or does, don't be afraid to speak with him or her about it. Stop by the teacher's room after class and share your feelings in a respectful way.

Understanding

Nobody Understands Me.

The ability to communicate is one of the most valuable skills anyone can learn. In one way or another, we spend most of our days communicating. During the school day, you interact with teachers, peers, older or younger kids, principals, cafeteria workers, librarians, and family members.

Believe it or not, to be better understood by people, you need to become a good listener. Listen to what people say with your ears, eyes, and heart. Try to understand the feelings behind their words. For example, one of your pals might say to you: "The music teacher is so mean. There's no way I'm trying out for chorus." You know she loves music, and she's been talking about trying out for the choir all year. So what's going on? If you listen well, you may figure out that she doesn't want to audition because she is afraid she won't get in. Taking the trouble to understand her will make any advice you give her much more helpful.

Making an effort to understand others improves your chances of being truly understood yourself. When friends, parents, or teachers see that you've taken the time to understand them, they will do the same for you.

Volunteer

How Can I Help?

We make contributions to our community when we help people out in meaningful ways. Service is the idea of giving back or saying thank-you for all the good things we have in our lives. You can get involved with service projects through school, church, synagogue, or social and community organizations. Many schools have a community service coordinator who organizes projects for interested students.

- ✓ Organize a pet-food drive for the animal shelter in your area.

- ✓ Stay after school with some friends and wash your teachers' blackboards.

- ✓ Pick up litter around your neighborhood or school.

- ✓ Make valentines for elderly people in a nursing home in your area.

- ✓ Collect children's books for the poor.

- ✓ Ask your family to donate time at a soup kitchen.

- ✓ Rake leaves for the elderly in your neighborhood.

- ✓ Walk a neighbor's dog.

- ✓ Read to little children.

- ✓ Collect canned goods for the poor.

- ✓ Offer an encouraging word to someone who is feeling down.

What If . . . .

There is so much life ahead of you. Strive to see the possibilities that life holds for you. Dream about your future. Feel free and brave to conjure up the most outlandish and exciting futures for yourself. Be hopeful and optimistic; the possibilities are limitless for you. All it takes is a dream and a spark.

Two girls I know want to open up their own ice cream store, and they are already testing out some very original flavors of ice cream. They believe they can do it. You may dream of playing violin with a symphony orchestra someday or working as part of a team of doctors that finds the cure for breast cancer. Dream the life and it can happen. Any accomplishment starts with the dream.

There are no boundaries or limitations to what girls can be and do. Girls are resilient and strong. Sustain the optimistic spirit of your girlhood past middle school into high school and college. As the world begins to see you in the body of a woman, remember that you can always tap the strength and power of the girl.

EXtracurricular

There's So Much to Do. I Can't Make up My Mind.

At the end of the day in elementary school, most of the kids you knew probably got on the bus and went home. There was the occasional roller-skating party in the gym or afternoon Girl Scout meeting, but that was pretty much the extent of after-school activities.

One of the best things about middle school is the wide array of extracurricular activities available to students. There are clubs, intramurals, and athletic teams to join or try out for. Most of the time these activities meet after school and are supervised or coached by teachers in your school. By getting involved in extracurricular activities at school, you'll meet kids who share similar interests. Read the school bulletin boards and listen to homeroom announcements about the offerings at your school. Here are some extracurricular activities that may interest you:

Art Club
Cheerleading
Chess Club
Chorus
Community Service
Dance Club
Drama Club
Foreign Language Clubs
Girl Scouts
Horseback-Riding Club
Intramural Sports
Math Club
Newspaper/Literary
    Magazine
Science Club
Ski Club
Sports Teams
Step Club
Student Government
Yearbook

$E=MC^2$

You Are the One!

What If They Don't Like Me?

There is no one in the entire world exactly like you. Isn't that exciting? Celebrate who you are. Be authentic. You are an original piece of artwork. It's not only okay to be different, it's great!

What's the use of trying to change yourself just so you can hang out with a certain group of kids? If you're trying to be someone or something you're not, it's just not going to feel right. Find the courage to be who you are. The longest-lasting friendships are based on honesty, and they blossom naturally.

It may not be easy at times. Peer pressure and the desire to fit in can be strong influences. But when you're true to yourself and your beliefs, you are always a winner.

Who Needs 'Em?

A disturbing phenomenon occurs during middle school. A lucky few will be able to breeze through with no problem, but the vast majority of teens have to learn to cope with this temporary annoyance. What am I talking about? ZITS!

Zits are caused when a pore in your skin becomes clogged with oil and then becomes infected by some bacteria. Most girls and boys experience zits between the ages of thirteen and seventeen. The most important thing you can do about it is to keep your skin clean. Wash your face in the morning and before you go to bed. Wash your hands frequently. You pick up all kinds of bacteria during the day that can be inadvertently transferred to your face. Keep your hair clean as well. Greasy or dirty hair that touches your face can transfer extra oil and bacteria to your skin. Zits can also break out on your back and shoulders. Be sure to keep those areas clean too.

Popping or picking at zits can cause permanent scars. Check out special soaps and creams sold to prevent zits or help them go away. If you have more severe skin problems, you may want to ask your parents to take you to a special skin doctor called a dermatologist. A dermatologist can prescribe stronger medications to help your skin improve.

What's the Word?

adolescence   The time of life between puberty and maturity.

algebra   A branch of mathematics where calculations are performed by means of letters, numbers, and symbols.

bacteria   Typically, one-celled micro-organisms that have no chlorophyll, multiply by simple division, and can be seen with a microscope. Some bacteria cause diseases such as pneumonia

bibliography   A list of sources of information on a given subject.

culture   The beliefs, social organizations, and way of life of a particular group of people.

hormones   Chemicals 'messengers' produced by organs in the body, that, among other things, trigger the onset of puberty.

independence   Freedom from the influence and control of another.

physiological   Pertaining to the functions and vital processes of the body.

procrastinate   To put off doing something until a later time.

puberty   The state of physical development when it first becomes possible to bear or conceive children.

pubic hair   Hair that covers the lower part of the abdomen surrounding the external genitals.

Campaign for Tobacco-Free Kids
1707 L Street NW
Washington, DC 20036
(800) 284-KIDS
Web site: http://www.tobaccofreekids.org

Association for Women in Science
1200 New York Avenue NW, Suite 650
Washington, D.C. 20005
(800) 886-2947
Web site: http://www.awis.org

4-H Council
7100 Connecticut Avenue
Chevy Chase, MD 20815
(301) 961-2840
Web site: http://www.fourhcouncil.edu

Girl Scouts of the U.S.A.
420 Fifth Avenue
New York, NY 10018-2798
(212) 852-8000

Girls Incorporated
120 Wall Street, 3rd floor
New York, NY 10005
(212) 509-2000
fax: (212) 509-8708

International Center for Research on Women
1717 Massachusetts Avenue NW
Washington, D.C. 20036
(202) 797-0007
Web site: http://www.icrw.org

Take Our Daughters to Work Day
Ms. Foundation for Women
120 Wall Street, 33rd floor
New York, NY 10005
(800) 676-7780
Web site: http://www.ms.foundation.org

Carlip, Hillary. *Girl Power: Young Women Speak Out.* New York: Warner Books, 1995.

Covey, Sean. *The 7 Habits of Highly Effective Teenagers.* New York: Simon and Schuster, 1998.

Gallop, Nancy. *Science Is Women's Work: Photos and Biographies of American Women in Sciences.* Windsor, CA: National History Project, 1993.

Gravelle, Karen, and Jennifer Gravelle. *The Period Book: Everything You Don't Want to Ask (But Need to Know).* New York: Walker, 1996.

Hart, Carol, Letty Cottin Pogrebin, Mary Rodgers, and Marlo Thomas. *Free to Be: You and Me.* New York: McGraw-Hill, 1998.

Jukes, Mavis. *It's a Girl Thing: How to Stay Healthy, Safe, and in Charge.* New York: Knopf, 1996.

On CD-ROM: *Let's Talk About Me: The Girl's Interactive Handbook for the 21st Century.* New York: Simon & Schuster, 1996.

Ms. Foundation for Women. *Girls Seen and Heard: 52 Life Lessons for Our Daughters.* New York: Penguin, 1998.

Perl, Teri. *Women and Numbers: Lives of Women Mathematicians.* San Carlo, CA: Wide World Publishing/Tetra, 1993.

Magazines

Girls' Life
4517 Harford Road
Baltimore, MD 21214
(410) 254-9200

New Girls Times
215 West 84th Street
New York, NY 10024
(212) 873-2132

New Moon Magazine
P.O. Box 3620
Duluth, MN 55803-3620
(800) 381-4743
Web site: http://www.newmoon.org

Index

About the Author

Jeanne Strazzabosco lives in Rochester, New York, where she teaches foreign languages at Pittsford Middle School. She is also a freelance writer who has written many books for young adults.

Photo Credits

Cover photo by Scott Bauer; pp. 6, 11, 17, 20, by Simca Israelian; p. 7 by Ira Fox; pp. 8, 12, 30, 31, 34, 36, by Thaddeus Harden; p. 14 by Steven Jones/FPG International; pp. 29, 32, 39, 40 © Skjold Photographs; pp. 30, 41 by Scott Bauer.

Design and Layout

Laura Murawski